Seneca Falls Library
47 Cayuga Street
Seneca Falls, NY 13148

American Idol
Host & Judges

ABDO
Publishing Company

by **Sarah Tieck**

VISIT US AT
www.abdopublishing.com

Published by ABDO Publishing Company, 8000 West 78th Street, Edina, Minnesota 55439.

Copyright © 2010 by Abdo Consulting Group, Inc. International copyrights reserved in all countries. No part of this book may be reproduced in any form without written permission from the publisher. Buddy Books™ is a trademark and logo of ABDO Publishing Company.

Printed in the United States of America, North Mankato, Minnesota.
112009
012010

 PRINTED ON RECYCLED PAPER

Coordinating Series Editor: Rochelle Baltzer
Contributing Editors: Heidi M.D. Elston, Megan M. Gunderson, BreAnn Rumsch, Marcia Zappa
Graphic Design: Maria Hosley
Cover Photograph: *Getty Images*: F Micelotta/American Idol 2009/Getty Images for Fox
Interior Photographs/Illustrations: *AP Photo*: Kevork Djansezian (pp. 8, 12, 27), Gretchen Ertl (p. 29), Mark Mainz (p. 15), Luis Martinez (p. 17), NBCU Photo Bank via AP Images (p. 7), Lucy Nicholson (p. 27), A. Rapoport/Picture Group (p. 11), Sipa via AP Images (p. 29), Mark J. Terrill (p. 27), Evans Vestal Ward/AP Images for Fox (p. 21), Vino Wong/Atlanta Journal Constitution (p. 23); *Getty Images*: David Livingston (p. 19), F Micelotta/American Idol 2009/Getty Images for Fox (p. 5), Charles Ommanney (p. 23), Kevin Winter (p. 24).

Library of Congress Cataloging-in-Publication Data

Tieck, Sarah, 1976-
  American idol host & judges / Sarah Tieck.
    p. cm. -- (Big buddy biographies)
  ISBN 978-1-60453-969-1
  1. American idol (Television program)--Juvenile literature. 2. Television personalities--United States--Biography--Juvenile literature. I. Title. II. Title: American idol host and judges.
  ML76.A54T54 2010
  791.45'72--dc22
                                2009035079

Contents

Star Makers

American Idol is a popular television show. Each season, talented young singers **compete** to be named the next American Idol.

Ryan Seacrest is the host of *American Idol*. Simon Cowell and Randy Jackson have been judges since the first season. Judge Kara DioGuardi joined the show in 2009.

For many years, Paula Abdul (*center*) was a judge on *American Idol*. She left the show before the 2010 season.

Tennessee

North Carolina

Atlanta ☆

South Carolina

Alabama Georgia

Florida

GULF OF MEXICO

ATLANTIC OCEAN

N
W E
S

Radio Days

Ryan John Seacrest was born in Atlanta, Georgia, on December 24, 1974. Ryan's parents are Connie and Gary Seacrest. He has a younger sister named Meredith.

Ryan has always been interested in hosting shows. Growing up, he would pretend to be a radio host. During high school, Ryan worked at a radio station. Then in college, he hosted a sports television show on ESPN.

From a young age, Ryan prepared himself to be a host. He learned radio and television skills and worked on his appearance.

Did you know...

For a while, Ryan studied journalism at the University of Georgia in Athens, Georgia.

As host of *American Idol*, Ryan introduces each singer. He also talks with them about their time on the show.

In 1994, Ryan moved to Los Angeles, California. There, his **career** grew. He hosted a popular radio show and became more well known.

In 2002, Ryan began hosting *American Idol*. This helped him gain fame and new opportunities.

Since then, Ryan has hosted important television shows. These include the *Emmy Awards* and *Dick Clark's New Year's Rockin' Eve*. He has also hosted the *American Top 40* radio show.

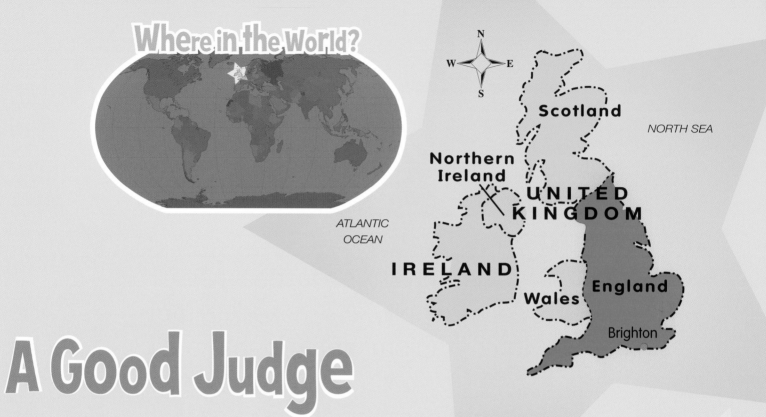

Where in the World?

N W E S

Scotland

NORTH SEA

Northern Ireland

UNITED KINGDOM

ATLANTIC OCEAN

IRELAND

Wales

England

Brighton

A Good Judge

Simon Phillip Cowell was born in Brighton, England, on October 7, 1959. Simon's parents are Julie Brett and Eric Cowell.

At age 16, Simon got a job in the mail room at EMI Music Publishing. In 1979, he began working with performers at the company. He knew then that he wanted to work in the music business.

Simon is known for his strong opinions.
Some people consider him a grouch.

For many years, Simon (*left*) was a judge with Paula (*center*) and Randy (*right*). They often disagreed about singers on the show.

Did you know...

Simon wrote a book about his life. It is called *I Don't Mean to be Rude, But....*

In 1985, Simon and a partner started Fanfare Records. But in 1989, the company closed. Simon kept working in the music business. In time, his **career** grew successful.

In 2001, Simon became a judge on the British show *Pop Idol*. Soon, he joined *American Idol*. He became known for telling the truth even when it hurt people's feelings. He wanted to help the singers improve. Simon soon began working on other shows, too.

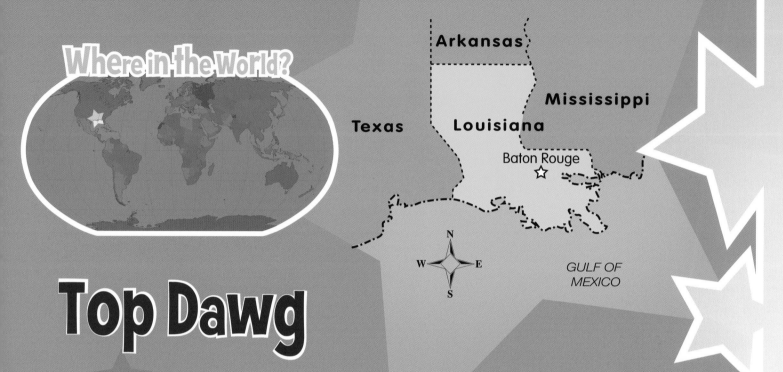

Arkansas

Mississippi

Texas Louisiana

Baton Rouge

GULF OF MEXICO

N
W E
S

Top Dawg

Randall "Randy" Jackson was born in Baton Rouge, Louisiana, on June 23, 1956. Randy's parents are Julia and Herman Jackson.

Growing up, Randy loved music. At age 13, he began playing the bass guitar. In high school, Randy joined a band. He took time off from college to work with famous musicians. Randy gained **experience** performing and became well known.

Randy has played music with famous singers and bands. They include Madonna, Elton John, and the band Journey.

During the 1990s, Randy worked for Columbia Records and MCA Records. His **career** grew more successful. He won a **Grammy Award** for his work as a **producer**.

By 2002, Randy had worked in the music business for more than 20 years. He was asked to use his knowledge as an *American Idol* judge. Since then, he's started hosting a radio show. He also produced a dance contest television show. It is called *America's Best Dance Crew*.

In 1999, Randy learned he had diabetes. During the early part of *American Idol*, Randy lost about 100 pounds (45 kg). This improved his health.

Big Break

Kara Elizabeth DioGuardi was born in Scarsdale, New York, on December 9, 1970. Kara's parents are Carol and Joseph J. DioGuardi. She has a younger brother named John.

Kara grew up in New Rochelle, New York. After college, she followed her interest in music. Kara discovered she had a talent for songwriting.

Sometimes, Kara performs her own songs or appears in music videos.

Did you know...

Kara's father was a congressman. Kara was also interested in politics. She studied political science at Duke University in Durham, North Carolina.

Kara has won awards for her songwriting.

Kara worked hard writing songs. Famous singers have recorded some of them. They include Kelly Clarkson, Carrie Underwood, and Jonas Brothers.

In 2009, Kara joined *American Idol* when it added a fourth judge. Kara continues to write songs. She also works for Warner Brothers Records.

Looking Back

American Idol started in 2002 as an American talent search. It was based on the British show Pop Idol.

Today, American Idol is one of the most popular television shows. Each season begins with young singers **auditioning** for the show. Judges choose a small group of finalists to perform.

The finalists sing each week. Then, viewers vote by phone to decide who stays on. The last person left is named the American Idol.

Millions of viewers watch *American Idol* from home. Some lucky fans get to watch the show live!

American Idol FRONT OF LINE

American Idol holds tryouts across the United States before each season begins. Thousands of singers line up to audition.

From 2002 to 2008, Randy, Paula, and Simon were the only judges.

For many years, Paula Abdul was one of three *American Idol* judges. She is an award-winning singer, dancer, and **choreographer**.

Paula was known for her kind, supportive comments. Her last season as a judge was in 2009.

Star Power

Every season, a new American Idol is chosen. The winner receives a record deal with a major recording company.

Many *American Idol* performers find success after the show. Some go on to record albums or **release** songs. Others star in movies or television shows. A few have even won **Grammy Awards**!

Jennifer Hudson did not win *American Idol*. But, she found success in music and movies.

Two of the most successful *American Idol* winners are Kelly Clarkson (*above*) and Carrie Underwood (*right*).

Ellen hadn't worked with singers before judging on *American Idol.* She hoped to be the voice of people who listen to music, such as fans.

Buzz

American Idol continues to be a successful show. In January 2010, the show's ninth season began. After tryouts, talk show host Ellen DeGeneres served as the fourth judge.

Fans are excited to see what's next for *American Idol*'s host and judges. Many believe they have bright **futures**!

Ellen hosts a talk show called *The Ellen DeGeneres Show*. She is known for being kind and funny.

Snapshot

★ **Names**: Ryan John Seacrest, Simon Phillip Cowell, Randall "Randy" Jackson, Kara Elizabeth DioGuardi

★ **Birthdays**: December 24, 1974 (Ryan), October 7, 1959 (Simon), June 23, 1956 (Randy), December 9, 1970 (Kara)

★ **Appearances Together**: *American Idol*

Important Words

audition (aw-DIH-shuhn) to give a trial performance showcasing personal talent as a musician, a singer, a dancer, or an actor.

career work a person does to earn money for a living.

choreographer (kawr-ee-AH-gruh-fuhr) someone who arranges the steps or movements of a dance.

compete to take part in a contest between two or more persons or groups.

experience skill or knowledge gained through practice or work.

future (FYOO-chuhr) a time that has not yet occurred.

Grammy Award any of the more than 100 awards given each year by the National Academy of Recording Arts and Sciences. Grammy Awards honor the year's best accomplishments in music.

producer a person who oversees the making of a movie, a play, an album, or a radio or television show.

release to make available to the public.

Web Sites

To learn more about the American Idol host & judges, visit ABDO Publishing Company online. Web sites about the American Idol host & judges are featured on our Book Links page. These links are routinely monitored and updated to provide the most current information available.

www.abdopublishing.com

Index